THE FROG BOOK

THE FROG BOOK

compiled and edited by

RICHARD SHAW

Illustrated

FREDERICK WARNE AND COMPANY, INC.
New York and London

ACKNOWLEDGMENTS

The editor and publishers wish to thank the following for their kind permission to reproduce copyrighted material used in this anthology. The publishers have made every effort to locate the owners of material used. If any omissions have been made, they offer their sincere apologies. Such omissions will be corrected in subsequent editions provided notification is sent to the publishers.

P. 12 "The Frog's Saddle Horse" from FOLK TALES OF ANGOLA, edited by Heli Chatelaine used by permission of the publisher, Houghton Mifflin Company. P.21 "How the Frog Lost His Tale," reprinted by permission of The World Publishing Company from AFRICAN VILLAGE FOLKTALES by Edna Mason Kaula. Copyright © 1968 by Edna Mason Kaula. P. 39 "The Frog," from CAUTIONARY VERSES, Hilaire Belloc. Published 1941 by Alfred A. Knopf, Inc. Reprinted by permission of the publisher. P. 46 "Haiku," from AN INTRODUCTION TO HAIKU by Harold G. Henderson. Copyright © 1958 by Harold G. Henderson. Reprinted by permission of Doubleday & Company, Inc. P. 48 "As the tadpole said . . ." by Ennis Rees. Reprinted from PUN FUN by Ennis Rees by permission of Abelard-Schuman, Ltd. All Rights Reserved. Copyright 1965.

Copyright © Frederick Warne & Co., Inc. 1972

Illustration on page 45 copyright © Ann Grifalconi 1972

All Rights Reserved

Manufactured in the United States of America

Library of Congress Catalog Card Number: 72-83128

ISBN 0 7232 6083 4

9205

Some people like frogs. Some people hate and fear them. Some people believe that frogs can bring rain, forecast the weather, soothe pain and cure diseases. But others believe that frogs are evil spirits born of the bones of a man-eating giant and that they cause eclipses by nibbling away at the moon.

There is one frog that begins life as a small pollywog and gradually grows up to the size of a small dog. The pollywog of another frog grows down, starting life as a huge ten-inch tadpole and shrinking to a peanut sized adult. Still another glides gracefully to earth from the treetops, using his webbed feet as a parachute. These are only three of the more than two hundred kinds of frogs scattered across the world, singing or croaking or grunting day and night.

But, large or small, good or evil, frogs have always been found on man's tables and altars, in his stories and myths and in his pictures and songs, happily croaking the time away.

THE ARTISTS WHO CREATED　　The illustrations are on
THE ILLUSTRATIONS ARE:　　　　the following pages:

John Ross—collagraph	(Frontispiece) 2
Randolph Caldecott—pen and ink	5, 18 and 29
Judith Gwyn Brown—crayon	7
Joseph Low—wash drawing	9
Rebecca Baxter—watercolor	11
Betula Margolis—pen and ink	13
Symeon Shimin—oil	23
Robert Galster—painted glass	26
Robin Kalin—magic marker	31
Kazue Mizumura—watercolor	35
Ismar David—pen and ink	40-41
Roger Duvoisin—watercolor collage	43
Ann Grifalconi—pen and ink	45
Yoko Mitsuhashi—watercolor	47
Paul Galdone—wash drawing	48

For Janet

The Frog

What a wonderful bird the frog are—
When he stand he sit almost;
When he hop, he fly almost.
He ain't go no sense hardly;
He ain't got no tail hardly either.
When he sit, he sit on what he ain't got almost.

—*Anonymous*

The Frog's Saddle Horse

Once upon a time the Elephant and the Frog went courting the same girl, and at last she promised to marry the Elephant. One day the Frog said to her: "That Elephant is nothing but my saddle horse."

When the Elephant came to call that night the girl said to him: "You are nothing but the Frog's saddle horse!"

When he heard this the Elephant went off at once and found the Frog, and asked him: "Did you tell the girl that I am nothing but your saddle horse?"

"Oh, no, indeed," said the Frog. "I never told her that!"

Thereupon they both started back together to see the girl. On the way the Frog said: "Grandpa Elephant, I am too tired to walk any further. Let me climb up on your back."

"Certainly," said the Elephant. "Climb up, my grandson." So the Frog climbed up on the Elephant's back. Presently he said: "Grandpa Elephant, I am afraid that I am going to fall off. Let me take some little cords and fasten them to your tusks, to hold on by."

"Certainly, my grandson," said the Elephant;

and he stood still while the Frog did as he had asked. Presently the Frog spoke again: "Grandpa Elephant, please stop and let me pick a green branch so that I can keep the flies off of you."

"Certainly, my grandson," said the Elephant, and he stood quite still while the Frog broke off the branch. Pretty soon they drew near to the house where the girl lived. And when she saw them coming, the Elephant plodding patiently along with the little Frog perched on his broad back, holding the cords in one hand and waving the green branch, she came to meet them, calling out: "Mr. Elephant, you certainly are nothing but the Frog's saddle horse!"

—*Angolan Folk Tale*

The Frogs Who Wished for a King

Down in the swamp
In a rushy, marshy bog
Lived some green-coated,
Yellow-vested,
Water-splashy frogs.
They stuck out their
      t o n g u e s,
Caught mosquitoes and flies,
Croaked great big
      b u r p s
And bulged out their eyes.
      BUT
Did they have fun?
Oh no! Not those frogs!
They were too busy
    kicking,
    hitting,
    scraaatching,
    biting,
Quarreling and fighting
Like a pack of wild dogs.

One day
A young frog named Greenie,
His thumbs in his jacket,
Cried, "Cool it, you frogs!
Stop all this racket!

Now gather around me,
Come on, form a huddle,
And soon you will see
How we can take the muddle
Out of this puddle
As easy as one-
 two-
 three!"
"How?" the frogs cried.
"Listen carefully," Greenie said.
"We need a King
With a crown on his head,
Who will rule us
 and school us,
And bring some pomp
To this swamp!"
"We wish for a KING!"
Cried the frogs to the skies.
 Then
 SWISH!

Down from the sky,
Through the mist,
Through the fog,
Zoomed a bumpety,
 lumpety,
Mossy old log.
 KERPLASH!

"Long live King Log!"
The frogs shouted.
"Hot-dog!
Now we'll have peace
In this marshy old bog."

And to celebrate, they
Dived off the lily pads,
Splashed in the pool,
Sunned on the royal log,
And acted the fool.
     BUT
Did they stay happy?
Oh no! Not those frogs!
They grumped
    harrumphed,
      groggled,
And griped.

"King Log is a fake," Greenie cried.
"He's a phony.
Calling him 'Your Majesty'
Is a lot of baloney.
He can't rule us,
    or school us,
    or govern our pool.
He's a stumpety,
    lumpety,
      bumpety fool.

"Come on, gang! Greenie shouted,
 "Let's try it once more.
Let's hear all you bullfrogs
Give out with a roar!"
"We wish for a REAL king!"
      Once again,
      SWISH!
Down from the sky,
Through the mist,
Swooped a stork.
His beak was as bright
And as sharp as a fork,
And that's how he used it—

To spear frogs for his lunch,
For dinner,
And Breakfast,
For snacktime or brunch.
"You wished for a king,"
Said the stork. "Here I am.
I'll expect you for tea—
With some crackers and jam."

The frogs kicked him
    and hit him.
They cried
"Who do you think . . .?"
    SNAPPETY-SLURP
    "Pass the mustard!"
They scratched him
    and bit him.
They screamed,
"A king's not supposed to . . ."
    GOBBLEDY-BURP
    "Where's the ketchup?"
Even for kicking,
    hitting,
    scraaatching,
    biting frogs,
It was a sad fate.
They had learned a hard lesson—
Too late.

A king who is cruel
May bring peace to your pool,
But what good will that do
If you're the
      meat
        for his
          stew?

But one frog escaped
Being bunned as a weenie.
From the rushes
Through the brush
And the brambles
Hopped Greenie.
And now on a lily pad
In a far-away pool
Greenie splashes and suns
And acts like a fool.
The mosquitoes and flies
Greenie finds quite delicious.
    BUT
He never fusses,
    or cusses
Or rouses the rabble.
He just soaks up the sunshine
And lets the brook babble.
    AND
He just never,
No NEVER,
Makes foolish wishes.

                        —*Kay McKemy (after Aesop)*

How the Frog Lost His Tale

Frog squatted in his muddy home on the edge of the water hole. He felt miserable. He knew he was ugly, with a mouth like a black cave and protruding eyes like doorknobs. And his figure! Frog worried because he thought he resembled nothing better than an old potato that has gone to seed. Frog's chief grievance was that he had no tail.

Each day at sundown when the forest and savanna animals came to drink, they swished their tails and jeered at Frog because he was ugly. So Frog went to the Sky God. He implored the great spirit to improve his appearance. "At least, give me a tail," Frog begged.

"Very well," the Sky God declared. "I will give you a tail if you will be watchman for my special well that never dries up."

Frog replied, "I will guard the well closely. Now, please, give me a tail."

Frog showed off his long, tapering tail by hopping to and fro before his new home beside the special well. Unfortunately, having such a magnificent tail as well as his responsible position made Frog conceited—and very bossy. And he never forgot or ever forgave the animals for their previous unfriendliness. Frog's arrogance became unbearable when every other water hole and well but his special charge dried up.

"Who comes to this muddy well?" Frog demanded when the animals crawled weakly in search of water to quench their thirst. Then he would shout rudely, "Go away! Go away! There is no water here. The well is dry."

The Sky God heard of Frog's behavior. He came quietly to the well and he received the same unkind treatment. The Sky God shook with anger. He punished Frog. He took away his tail and he drove him from the well.

The Sky God keeps reminding Frog of the misery he caused. Every springtime when Frog is born as a tadpole, he has a long, beautiful tail. But as he grows, his tail shrinks. It shrinks and shrinks and then it disappears.

The Sky God takes the tail away because Frog was once spiteful and unforgiving.

—*Bantu Folk Tale*

A Legend of Lake Okeefinokee

There once was a frog,
And he lived in a bog,
On the banks of Lake Okeefinokee,
And the words of the song
That he sang all day long
Were, "Croakety croakety croaky."

Said the frog, "I have found
That my life's daily round
In this place is exceedingly poky.
So no longer I'll stop,
But I swiftly will hop
Away from Lake Okeefinokee."

Now a bad mocking-bird
By mischance overheard
The words of the frog as he spokee,
And he said, "All my life
Frog and I've been at strife,
As we lived by Lake Okeefinokee.

"Now I see at a glance
Here's a capital chance
For to play him a practical jokee.
So I'll venture to say
That he shall not today
Leave the banks of Lake Okeefinokee."

So this bad mocking-bird,
Without saying a word,
He flew to a tree which was oaky;
And loudly he sang,
Till the whole forest rang,
"Oh! Croakety croakety croaky!"

As he warbled this song,
Master frog came along,
A-filling his pipe for to smokee;
And he said, " 'Tis some frog
Has escaped from the bog
Of Okeefinokee-finokee.

"I am filled with amaze
To hear one of my race
A-warbling on top of an oaky;
But if frogs can climb trees,
I may still find some ease
On the banks of Lake Okeefinokee."

So he climbed up the tree;
But alas! down fell he!
And his lovely green neck it was brokee;
And the sad truth to say,
Nevermore did he stray
From the banks of Lake Okeefinokee.

And the bad mocking-bird
Said, "How very absurd
And delightful a practical jokee!"
But I'm happy to say
He was drowned the next day
In the waters of Okeefinokee.

—*Laura E. Richards*

The Frog and the Ox

A Very Small Frog— so small that he was a tadpole just last week— plopped into the water of the Placid Pool. He swam quickly towards a Very Big Frog sunning himself on a lily pad.

"Daddy!" cried the Very Small Frog, "I have just seen a mighty monster, big as a house, with horns on his head and two pointed toes on each foot."

"That was only Farmer Brown's ox, and he's not so big," said the Very Big Frog. "He may be just a bit taller than I am, but I can make myself just as wide."

And with that, the Very Big Frog took a very deep breath and asked, "Was he as wide as this?"

"Much, much wider," said the Very Small Frog.

So the Very Big Frog took two more very deep breaths and gasped, "Was he as wide as this?"

"Much, much, much wider," said the Very Small Frog.

Then the Very Big Frog took three more very deep breaths and wheezed, "Was he as wide as . . ."

But before he could finish, he burst with a loud pop!

If you try to be something you are not, you may end up being nothing.

—Aesop

Afternoon by a Pond
in the Heart of Vermont

This pond is a window which the sun lights up.
Submerged, under glass, lie the frogs. They are green.
In suggestions of emerald, onyxes, golds,
They move, as in a dream, near the water-lily's cup;
Oddly, they float, only half half-seen,
Their eyes like the shield that Perseus holds.

The gauze wings of dragonflies pennant the air;
The shadows of falcons are sewn on the water
And the shapes in its moat dive down; all goes blind;
Where are the frogs whose disguisings compare
Them to a king's, caught, enchanted daughter,
Or to wizards whose capes are boldly designed

With spells? The cleared water settles,
The hawks disappear into legends of sky.
The pond, under glass, goes to jewel; lights refract;
The dusk dims down in a fragrance of petals
And hushes the world in the mind of the eye
Until singing takes hold, turning frogs into fact.

—*Joan Hutton*

The Frog

Once upon a time there was a woman who had three sons. Though they were peasants they were well off, for the soil on which they lived was fruitful, and yielded rich crops. One day they all three told their mother they meant to get married. To which their mother replied, "Do as you like, but see that you choose good housewives, who will look carefully after your affairs; and to make certain of this, take with you these three skeins of flax, and give it to them to spin. Whoever spins the best will be my favourite daughter-in-law."

Now the two eldest sons had already chosen their wives; so they took the flax from their mother, and carried it off with them, to have it spun as she had said. But the youngest son was puzzled what to do with his skein, as he knew no girl (never having spoken to any) to whom he could give it to be spun. He wandered hither and thither, asking the girls that he met if they would undertake the task for him, but at the sight of the flax they laughed in his face and mocked at him. Then in despair he left their villages, and went out into the country, and, seating himself on the bank of a pond, began to cry bitterly.

Suddenly there was a noise close beside him, and a frog jumped out of the water on to the bank, and asked him why he was crying. The youth told her of his trouble, and how his brothers would bring home linen spun for them by their promised wives, but that no one would spin his thread.

Then the frog answered, "Do not weep on that account; give me the thread, and I will spin it for you." And, having said this, she took it out of his hand, and flopped back into the water, and the youth went back home not knowing what would happen next.

In a short time the two elder brothers came home, and their mother asked to see the linen which had been woven out of the skeins of flax she had given them. They all three left the room; and in a few minutes the two eldest returned, bringing with them the linen that had been spun by their chosen wives. But the youngest brother was greatly troubled, for he had nothing to show for the skein of flax that had been given him. Sadly he betook himself to the pond, and sitting down on the bank, began to weep.

Flop! and the frog appeared out of the water close beside him.

"Take this," she said. "Here is the linen I have spun for you."

You may imagine how delighted the youth was. She put the linen into his hands, and he took it straight back to his mother, who was so pleased with it that she declared she had never seen linen so beautifully spun, and that it was far finer and whiter than the webs that the two elder brothers had brought home.

Then she turned to her sons and said, "But this is not enough, my sons, I must have another proof of what sort of wives you have chosen. In the house there are three puppies. Each of you take one, and give it to the woman whom you mean to bring home as your wife. She must train it and bring it up. Whichever dog turns out the best, its mistress will be my favourite daughter-in-law."

So the young men set out on their different ways, each taking a puppy with him. The youngest, not knowing where to go, returned to the pond, sat down once more on the bank and began to weep.

Flop! and close beside him he saw the frog. "Why are you weeping?" she said.

Then he told her his difficulty, and that he did not know to whom he should take the puppy.

"Give it to me," she said, "and I will bring it up for you." And, seeing that the youth hesitated, she took the little creature out of his arms, and disappeared with it into the pond.

The weeks and the months passed, till one day the mother said she would like to see how the dogs had been trained by her future daughters-in-law. The two eldest sons departed, and returned shortly, leading with them two great mastiffs, who growled

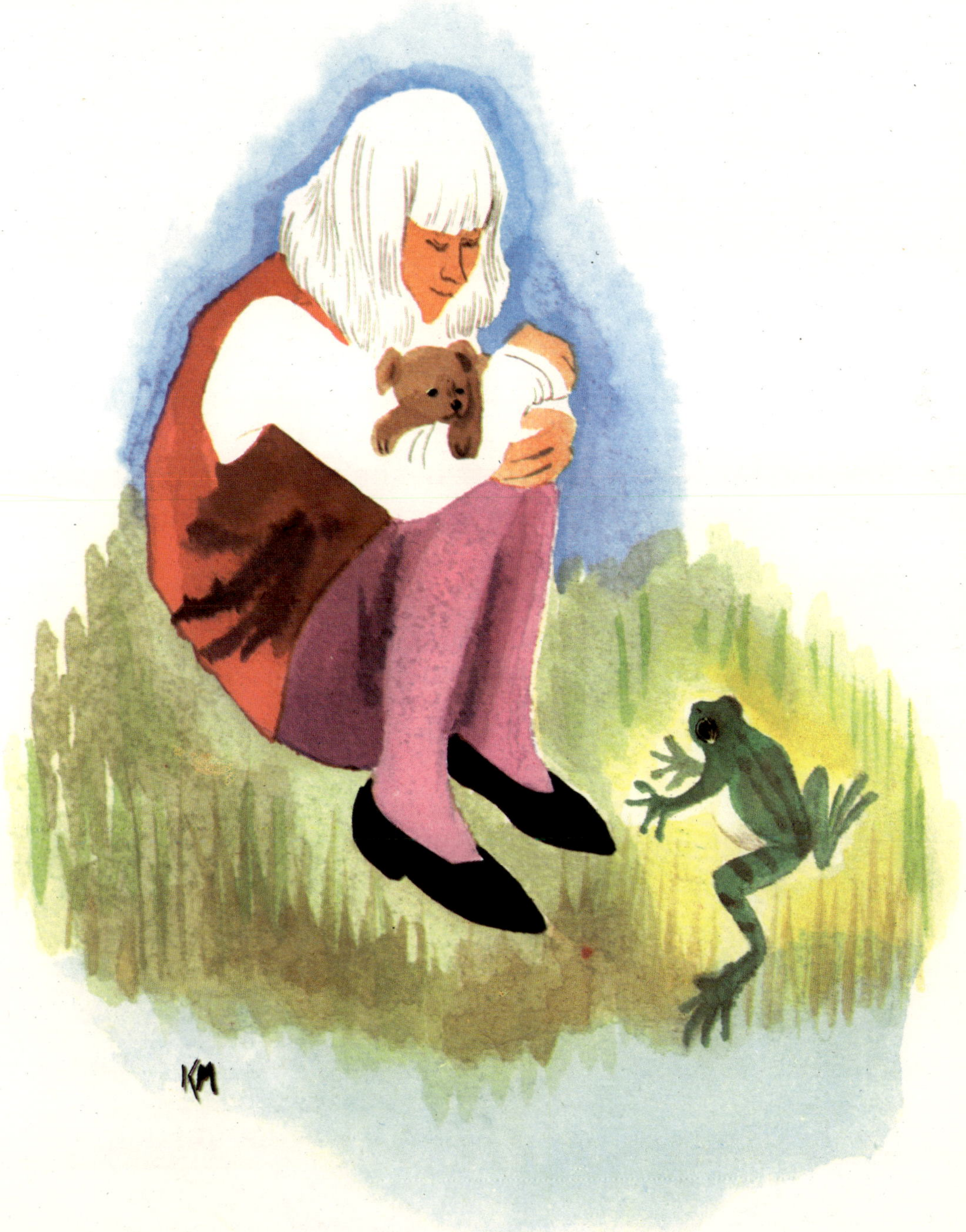

so fiercely, and looked so savage, that the mere sight of them made the mother tremble with fear.

The youngest son, as was his custom, went to the pond, and called on the frog to come to his rescue.

In a minute she was at his side, bringing with her the most lovely little dog, which she put into his arms. It sat up and begged with its paws, and went through the prettiest tricks, and was almost human in the way it understood and did what it was told.

In high spirits the youth carried it off to his mother. As soon as she saw it, she exclaimed, "This is the most beautiful little dog I have ever seen. You are indeed fortunate my son; you have won a pearl of a wife."

Then, turning to the others, she said, "Here are three shirts; take them to your chosen wives. Whoever sews the best will be my favourite daughter-in-law."

So the young men set out once more; and again, this time, the work of the frog was much the best and neatest.

This time the mother said, "Now that I am content with the tests I gave, I want you to go and fetch home your brides, and I will prepare the wedding-feast."

You may imagine what the youngest brother felt on hearing these words. Whence was he to fetch a bride? Would the frog be able to help him in this new difficulty? With bowed head, and feeling very sad he sat down on the edge of the pond.

Flop! and once more the faithful frog was beside him.

"What is troubling you so much?" she asked him. And then the youth told her everything.

"Will you take me for a wife?" she asked.

"What should I do with you as a wife?" he replied, wondering at her strange proposal.

"Once more, will you have me, or will you not?" she said.

"I will neither have you, nor will I refuse you," said he.

At this the frog disappeared; and the next minute the youth beheld a lovely little chariot, drawn by two tiny ponies, standing on the road. The frog was holding the carriage door open for him to step in.

"Come with me," she said. And he got up and followed her into the chariot.

As they drove along the road they met three witches; the first of them was blind, the second was hunchbacked, and the third had a large thorn in her throat. When the witches beheld the chariot, with the frog seated pompously among the cushions, they broke into such fits of laughter that the eyelids of the blind one burst open, and she recovered her sight;

the hunchback rolled about on the ground in merriment till her back became straight, and in a roar of laughter the thorn fell out of the throat of the third witch.

And now the witches' first thought was to reward the frog, who had been the means of curing their misfortunes. The first witch waved her magic wand over the frog, and changed her into the loveliest girl that had ever been seen. The second witch waved the wand over the tiny chariot and ponies, and they turned into a beautiful large carriage with prancing horses and a coachman on the seat. The third witch gave the girl a magic purse that would be always filled with money.

Having done this, the witches disappeared, and the youth with his lovely bride drove to his mother's home. Great was the delight of the mother at her youngest son's good fortune. A beautiful house was built for them; she was the favourite daughter-in-law; everything went well with them, and they lived happily ever after.

—*Leonora Alleyne*

The Frog

Be kind and tender to the Frog,
    And do not call him names,
As 'Slimy skin' or 'Polly-wog,'
    Or likewise 'Ugly James,'
Or 'Gap-a-grin,' or 'Toad-gone-wrong,'
    Or 'Bill Bandy Knees':
The Frog is justly sensitive
    To epithets like these.

No animal will more repay
    A treatment kind and fair,
At least so lonely people say
Who keep a frog (and by the way,
    They are extremely rare).

        —*Hilaire Belloc*

Twenty Froggies

Twenty froggies went to school
Down beside a rushy pool,—
Twenty little coats of green,
Twenty vests all white and clean.

"We must be in time," said they:
"First we study, then we play:
That is how we keep the rule,
When we froggies go to school."

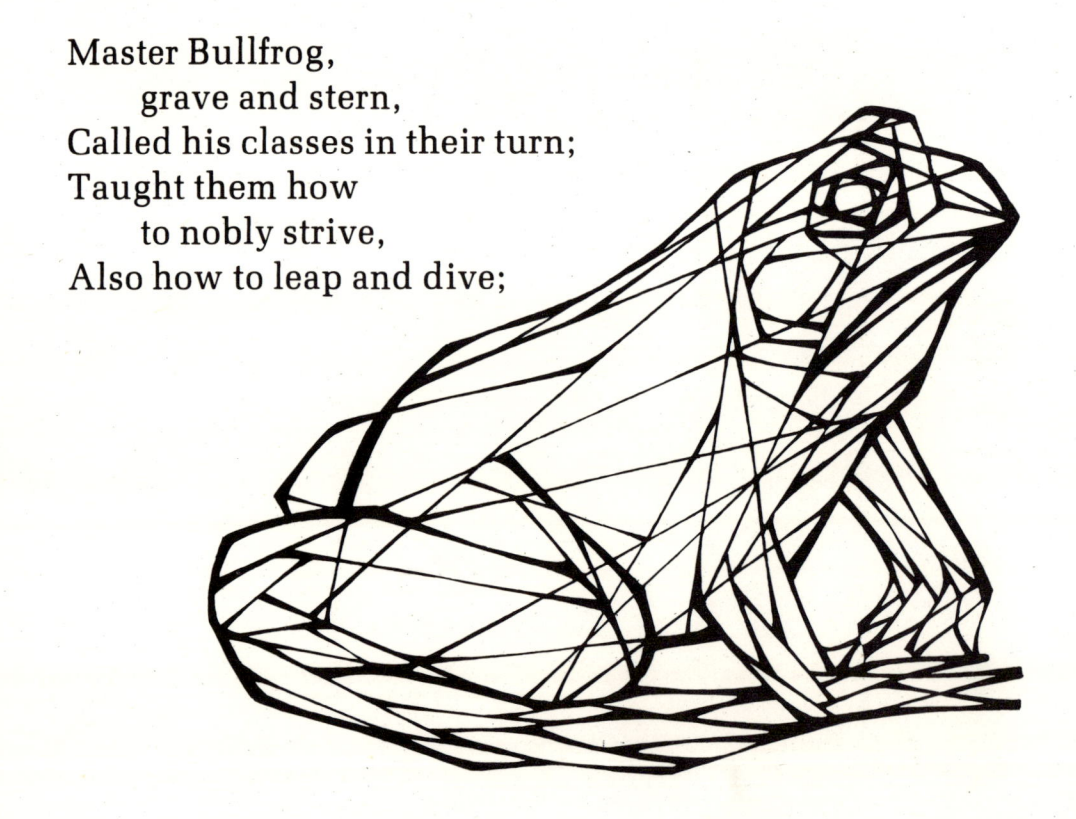

Master Bullfrog,
    grave and stern,
Called his classes in their turn;
Taught them how
    to nobly strive,
Also how to leap and dive;

From his seat upon a log,
Showed them how
    to say, "Ker-chog!"
Also how to dodge a blow
From the sticks that bad boys throw.

Twenty froggies grew up fast;
Bullfrogs they became at last.
Not one dunce was in the lot,
Not one lesson they forgot.

Polished in a high degree,
As each froggie ought to be,
Now they sit on other logs
Teaching other little frogs.

—George Cooper

The Frog

Behold the Frog, and then Contrast
His Present with his Humble Past!
Once but a Tadpole in a Pool,
Now nature's gayly Painted Fool.
So *Newly Rich* in Legs and Toes,
He's sadly lacking in Repose,
Yet He is never Impolite.
He hops and jumps from sheer delight,
And shows with each Gymnastic Spasm
The Convert's Fresh Enthusiasm.

—Oliver Herford

Hopping Frog

Hopping frog, hop here and be seen,
    I'll not pelt you with stick or stone:
Your cape is laced and your coat is green;
    Goodbye, we'll let each other alone.

—Christina Rossetti

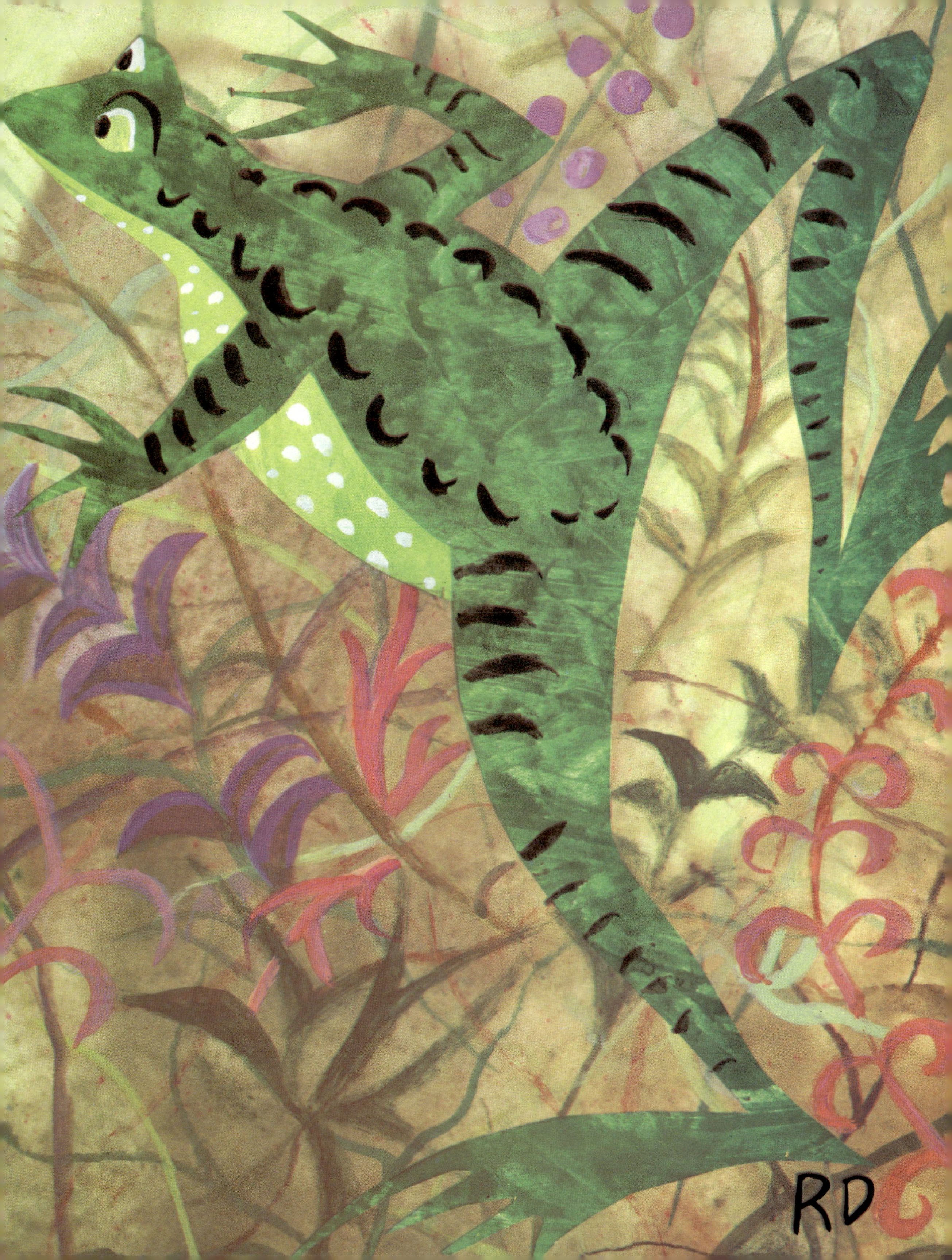
RD

Who But a Tadpole?

There are people who envy
The elephant's strength,
The song of the lark,
The whale for his length.

There are people who envy
The bee for his sting,
The mink for his coat,
The panther his spring.

There are people who envy
The heron his beak,
The monkey his tail,
The bull his physique.

There are people who envy
The ways of a hog,
But who but a tadpole
Would envy a frog?

—*Richard Shaw*

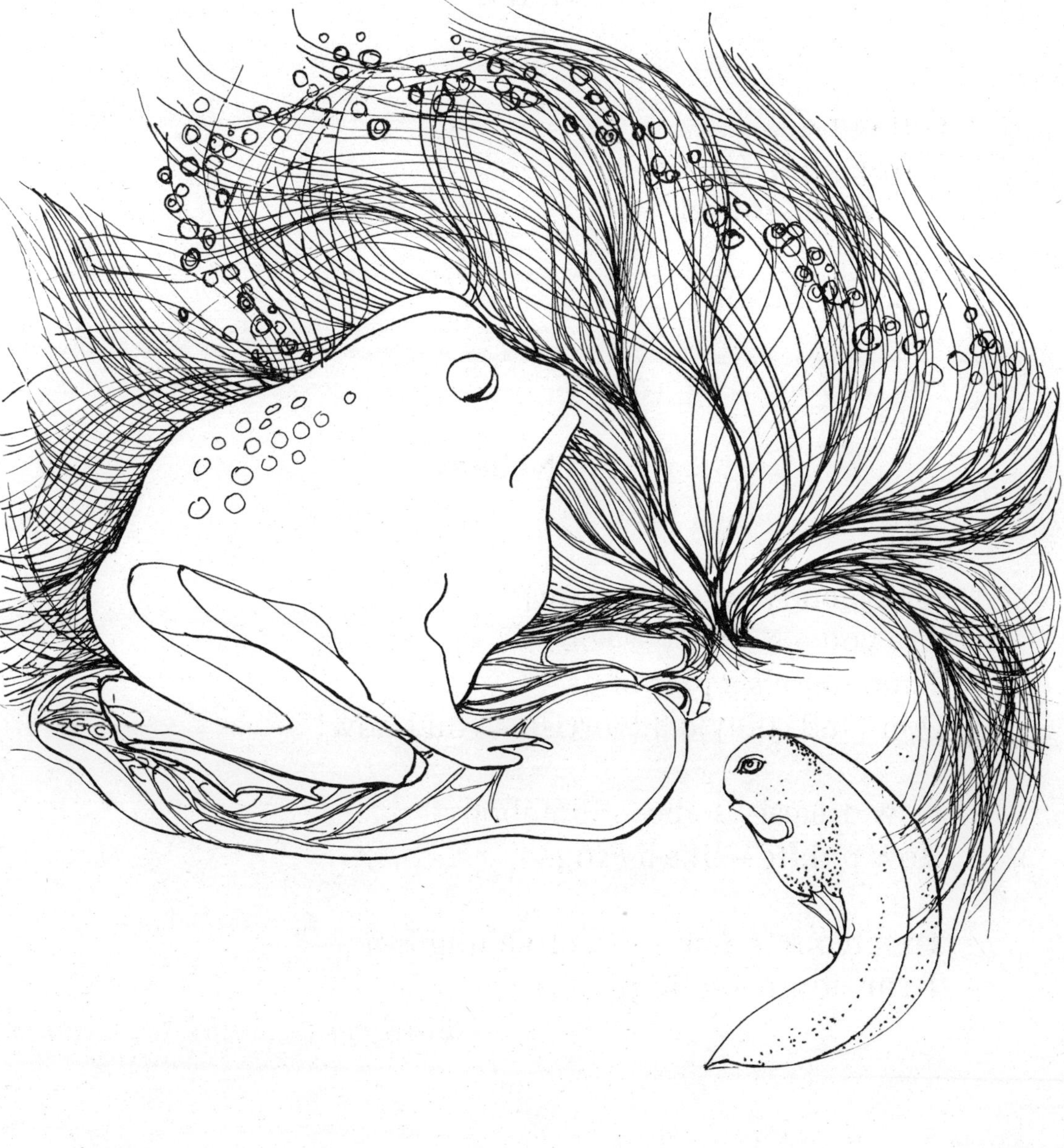

Haiku

Old pond:
   frog jump in
      water-sound.

—Basho

I'm Nobody

I'm Nobody! Who are you?
Are you—Nobody—Too?
Then there's a pair of us?
Don't tell! they'd advertise—you know!

How dreary—to be—Somebody!
How public—like a Frog—

To tell one's name—the livelong June—
To an admiring Bog!
                —Emily Dickinson

Yoko Mitsuhashi

As the Tadpole Said

As the tadpole said
From under the log,
"My tale is ended,
And now I'm a frog."

—Ennis Rees